Dear Daughter

Favorite Writings

About the Joys

of Daughters

Selected by

Peter Seymour

Illustrated by

Carolyn Pickett

HALLMARK EDITIONS

Contents

Paul Engle A Radiance of Daughters

One summer afternoon when my daughter was five years old I took her with me to follow the working of a mole which had been happily tunneling around our backyard. She looked at the low upheavings of the grass for a moment and then asked, "What did it?"

"A little animal called a mole," I told her.

She considered that doubtfully, and then her face brightened as she exclaimed, "Then it must be an animole!"

The discovery of language is one of a child's greatest experiences, perhaps more so for a daughter than for a son. A boy is much more likely to *act* in a situation, while a girl in the same scene would more likely speak, especially if it is an event to which the young male would respond with violence.

This same relationship between language and a daughter has affected many writers. When they have written about the little girls inhabiting their house (no, not inhabiting, but giving a radiance to the house), even their prose style has become livelier.

Having written an entire volume of sonnets about my two daughters, I know intensely the love of a daughter for language, and the response that it in turn brings out in a writer-father. In her poem "Prayer for a Daughter," Esther Wood ends with a line any writer would honor: "Don't forget to give her winter." That is to say, be sure she knows the darkness and bitter cold of life as well as its warmth and sweetness.

Say the word "daughter," slowly, prolong its gentle sound. Notice the way it lingers on the tongue like a piece of candy. Then speak the word "son." Doesn't it have, like the masculine creature it names, a greater hardness? Doesn't it disappear from the mouth in the moment of its uttering? In such a difference of simple nouns there is contained the quality of actual difference between the girl and the boy. That distinction carries over into writing about children too, as many examples in this book prove.

A good daughter is like a good piece of writing: candid, lyrical, graceful, moving, alive. I have seen a young girl walk across a room, intent on her intense errand, and it was like seeing a voice become visible, as if not her tongue but her motion said, "I will do this for my life."

WELCOME,

DAUGHTER

What Is A Girl?

Little girls are the nicest things that happen to people. They are born with a little bit of angel-shine about them and though it wears thin sometimes, there is always enough left to lasso your heart—even when they are sitting in the mud, or crying temperamental tears, or parading up the street in mother's best clothes.

A little girl can be sweeter (and badder) oftener than anyone else in the world. She can jitter around, and stomp, and make funny noises that frazzle your nerves, yet just when you open your mouth, she stands there demure with that special look in her eyes. A girl is Innocence playing in the mud, Beauty standing on its head, and Motherhood dragging a doll by the foot.

Girls are available in five colors—black, white, red, yellow, or brown, yet Mother Nature always manages to select your favorite color when you place your order. They disprove the law of supply and demand—there are millions of little girls, but each is as precious as rubies.

God borrows from many creatures to make a little girl. He uses the song of a bird, the squeal of a pig, the stubbornness of a mule, the antics of a monkey, the spryness of a grasshopper, the curiosity of a cat, the speed of a gazelle, the slyness of a fox, the softness of a kitten, and to top it all off He adds the mysterious mind of a woman.

A little girl likes new shoes, party dresses, small animals, first grade, noise makers, the girl next door, dolls, make-believe, dancing lessons, ice cream, kitchens, coloring books, make-up, cans of water, going visiting, tea parties, and one boy. She doesn't care so much for visitors, boys in general, large dogs, hand-me-downs, straight chairs, vegetables, snow suits, or staying in the front yard. She is loudest when you are thinking, the prettiest when she has provoked you, the busiest at bedtime, the quietest when you want her to show off, and the most flirtatious when she absolutely must not get the best of you again.

Who else can cause you more grief, joy, irritation, satisfaction, embarrassment, and genuine delight than this combination of Eve, Salome, and Florence Nightingale? She can muss up your home, your hair, and your dignity— spend your money, your time, and your temper —then just when your patience is ready to crack, her sunshine peeks through and you've lost again.

Yes, she is a nerve-wracking nuisance, just a noisy bundle of mischief. But when your dreams tumble down and the world is a mess—when it seems you are pretty much of a fool after all—she can make you a king when she climbs on your knee and whispers, "I love you best of all!"

Alan Beck

Recognition

"I don't want to hear another word!"
I hear my daughter scold.
"Dear me!" I think, "She's awfully strict
For a playful three-year-old!"
She rolls her big eyes heavenward
And sighs with great disdain
"What am I going to do with you?"
Her dolls hear her complain.
"Sit down! Be still! Hold out your hands!
Do you have to walk so slow?
Pick up your toys! Go brush your teeth!
Eat all your carrots! Blow!"
I start to tell her how gentle
A mother ought to be
When blushingly, I realize
She's imitating me!

Barbara Burrow

A Small Daughter Walking Outdoors

Easy, wind!
Go softly here!
She is small
And very dear.

She is young
And cannot say
Words to chase
The wind away.

She is new
To walking, so
Wind, be kind
And gently blow

On her ruffled head,
On grass and clover.
Easy, wind . . .
She'll tumble over!

Frances Frost

A Father's Love

Certain it is that there is no kind of affection so purely angelic as that of a father to a daughter. He beholds her both with and without regard to her sex. In love to our wives there is desire; to our sons there is ambition; but in that to our daughters there is something which there are no words to express. *Joseph Addison*

To a Daughter Nine Months Old

As a correspondent in France during World War I, Richard Harding Davis wrote this tongue-in-cheek letter home to his daughter Hope, who had been born the previous January: So many weeks have passed since I saw you that by now you are able to read this without your mother looking over your shoulder and helping you with the big words. I have six sets of pictures of you. Every day I take them down and change them. Those your dear mother put in glass frames I do not change. Also, I have all the sweet fruits and chocolates and red bananas. How good of you to think of just the things your father likes. . . .

Be very good. Do not bump yourself. Do not eat matches. Do not play with scissors or cats. Do not forget your dad. Sleep when your mother wishes it. Love us both. Try to know how we love you. That you will never learn. Goodnight and God keep you, and bless you.

Richard Harding Davis

Now She Becomes a World of Words

Now she becomes a world
Of words: the furious *I*,
The us like an arm curled
Over her shoulder, cry
Of the demanding me,
The angry yell of you,
The loving word for we,
The questioning of who?

For saying makes things real:
Ouch! is the cause of pain,
Wet is the taste of rain,
Cut is the noun for knife,
Pig is the pride of squeal,
Child is the look of life.

Paul Engle

The Beginning

"Where have I come from, where did you pick me up?" the baby asked its mother.

She, half crying, half laughing, and clasping the baby to her breast,—

"You were hidden in my heart as its desire, my darling.

"You were in the dolls of my childhood's games; and when with clay I made the image of my god every morning, I made and unmade you then. . . .

"In all my hopes and my loves, in my life, in the life of my mother, you have lived.

"In the lap of the deathless Spirit who rules our home you have been nursed for ages.

"When in girlhood my heart was opening its petals, you hovered as a fragrance about it. . . .

"Heaven's first darling, twin-born with the morning light, you have floated down the stream of the world's life, and at last you have stranded on my heart.

"As I gaze on your face, mystery overwhelms me: you who belong to all have become mine.

"For fear of losing you I hold you tight to my breast. What magic has snared the world's treasure in these slender arms of mine?"

Rabindranath Tagore

Who Is Sylvia?

How many daughters suffer under first names bestowed upon them by loving parents which they consider unattractive or inconvenient? Here author Sylvia Wright speaks for them all: I first became aware of the cross I bear when I was a very small child, playing in a wood in Berkeley, California, in a garment called a "nature suit." This is not what it sounds like, but a one-piece gingham play suit with longish shorts and straps over the shoulders trimmed with rickrack. At the time it was considered advanced, but healthy.

My mother and a strange lady encountered me and my mother introduced me. The strange lady looked misty and said, "Ah, yes, a wood nymph."

I was told this was the meaning of my name, and I promptly became a wood nymph. I enjoyed it enormously, but shortly thereafter for the first time in my life I took a realizing sense of myself in a long mirror. I did not see an ethereal fairy-like sprite in flowing pale-green draperies. I saw a small, solemn-looking, tubby, rufous (straight-haired) blonde in a wrinkled nature suit. My yells of rage and disillusionment were heart-rending. . . .

People in Cambridge, Massachusetts, where my grandparents lived, assumed that I was named after a figment of my grandmother's imagination. My grandmother was a novelist; she fell under the sway of the name; and she wrote a novel that had not one, but two Sylvias. She had the inestimable grace to create a heroine (the main Sylvia) who was thirty-eight and had snow-white hair (a wealth), and to let her, in the end, win the charming scholarly hero from a younger and more dynamic lady. But she couldn't resist making her "ethereal," "delicate," "transparently pale." They laughed when they asked if I were named for her.

In actual fact my mother irresponsibly named me after a little English girl she had met while traveling. The English girl had a younger sister named Phyllis, and neatly enough, my mother produced a Phyllis about three years after me. Bad as it was to be named Sylvia, it was worse to have Phyllis trailing after you, equally tubby, unspritelike, and not even pastoral-looking.

When we complained, my mother added insult to injury by explaining that in each case she had been somewhat at a loss for a name because she was confidently expecting Benjamin. She said she herself had always suffered because people kept asking her, ha, ha, if she thought she had married the Wright man.

My older brother called me "Saliva."

Sylvia Wright

THE DELIGHTS

OF LITTLE GIRLS

Spring

At the age of ten, in 1904, Virginia Cary Hudson wrote a number of essays for a favorite teacher at her Episcopalian boarding school. "Spring" puckishly sums up the attitudes of any daughter in those years before she becomes a woman:

Spring is beautiful, and smells sweet. Spring is when you shake the curtains, and pound on the rugs, and take off your long underwear, and wash in all the corners. Spring is when the carpet tacks come up, and all the blinds come down. In the Spring horses and mules have colts, and Tillie Unger has a baby. The doctor says "goodbye until next year." The priest says "how very sweet." And my grandmother says "how perfectly horrible."

The best thing about Spring is Easter and your new hat. Mine comes from Best & Co. My hat always has a ribbon. I will be glad when I am 14 and can have a flower. One time my ribbon is white. One time it is blue. I like red, but my mother says no. Mrs. Daniels has a beautiful pink rose on her hat. She sprays rose perfume on her rose, and after church she lets me smell it. I bet if she walked home instead of riding, a big bee would follow her all the way.

I like bees. I hunt for them and slap them down with my base ball mitt. Then I mash them and put them in a bottle. When I have ten, Nelson Brady has to give me his best agate.

Spring is when you draw a circle in the dirt with your finger, if you don't have a stick, and win all of the boys' marbles. My mother rubs lemon on her hands to make them white. I rub salt on my shooting thumb to make it tough. Spring is when you put ladders up high and scrape out gutters, and when you put ladders down low and clean out cisterns.

I had a very good idea that Mr. Hamilton was going to find a tom cat in his cistern. Oscar Sargent bet me my whole bag of gum drops that Miss Nelly McDonnell's cat couldn't scratch himself out if we buried him. I bet he could. But if he could, he didn't. Oscar says to me, he says, "What do people do with dead bodies?" And I said to Oscar, "they tie rocks on them and throw them in the river." And Oscar says, "but we don't have a river." And I said, "Mr. Hamilton has the biggest, deepest cistern in town." And now if Oscar says I told him to put Miss Nelly's tom cat in Mr. Hamilton's cistern, he is just adding up 2 and 2 and getting five. Miss Nelly bought a can of salmon and called Kitty, Kitty the whole long day.

Spring is when the sap comes up and the flowers start blooming and the young men start up their courting. If they are poor, they walk you up one side of the street and down the other. But if they have money, and are not stingy, they come for you in a high buggy and put a linen duster on your lap.

I can't find out one thing from people except about geography, and arithmetic, and etiquette, and religion. I can't find out a thing about courting. I sure will feel silly if anybody ever comes courting me. I asked my mother what I should talk about while I was courting. She said not to worry, she felt sure I would not be "lacking in conversation" whatever that means. When I have my children, if I ever learn anything about courting, I am going to tell them what they ask me. I am going to answer all my children's questions and not start up that sniffing, and rolling my eyes like my mother does. . . .

Virginia Cary Hudson

Oh, my son's my son till he gets him a wife,
But my daughter's my daughter all her life.

Dinah Craik

An Obedient Daughter

For a little while, I remember, Lorli had attended a kindergarten in Salzburg. There she had made the fatal acquaintance of scissors and learned what wonderful patterns you can cut out of a folded piece of paper. The first item on which she tried it was her beautiful, new, fluffy pink blanket. I admonished her earnestly never to do that again. She promised, and must have meant, never again on a blanket, because the next victim was one of the precious brocade curtains in the living room. Now she was told that under no circumstances might those scissors cut anything which was not strictly her private property. She promised, and looked, oh, so sincere. Her left hand took a firm grip on the curls above her forehead, and before I could cry "no," the scissors had cut what was strictly her own. But she hadn't disobeyed.

When she started going to school, she never came home. Hours passed every day, and I got worried. So, I explained to her she must always keep going and never stop. The very next day I was waiting again, and finally I went all the way into town to find her walking up and down, chatting cheerily with a policeman, who said to me when I took hold of my daughter:

"Your little girl kept me very nice company. She said I should walk up and down with her because she wasn't supposed to stop, and she told me all about her home."

That I could believe.   *Maria Augusta Trapp*

To His Daughter From in Prison

In prison for embezzlement, the man who would become the famous author O. Henry wrote to his young daughter Margaret:

Hello, Margaret:

Don't you remember me? I'm a Brownie, and my name is Aldibirontiphostiphornikophokos. If you see a star shoot and say my name seventeen times before it goes out, you will find a diamond ring in the track of the first blue cow's foot you see go down the road in a snowstorm while the red roses are blooming on the tomato vines. Try it some time. I know all about Anna and Arthur Dudley, but they don't see me. I was riding by on a squirrel the other day and saw you and Arthur Dudley give some fruit to some trainmen. Anna wouldn't come out. Well good-bye, I've got to take a ride on a grasshopper. I'll just sign my first letter—"A."

A Letter To Lucy

Sydney Smith was one of the funniest men alive in the time of Charles Dickens, and was much sought after for his wit. A decade before his death he wrote this famous letter to his daughter Lucy, who was traveling at the time:

Lucy, Lucy, my dear child, don't tear your frock: tearing frocks is not in itself a proof of genius; but write as your mother writes, act as your mother acts; be frank, loyal, affectionate, simple, honest; and then integrity or laceration of frock is of little import.

And Lucy, dear child, mind your arithmetic. You know, in the first sum of yours I ever saw, there was a mistake. You had carried two (as a cab is licensed to do) and you ought, dear Lucy, to have carried but one. Is this a trifle? What would life be without arithmetic, but a scene of horrors?

You are going to Boulogne, the city of debts, peopled by men who never understood arithmetic; by the time you return, I shall probably have received my first paralytic stroke, and shall have lost all recollection of you; therefore I now give you my parting advice. Don't marry anybody who has not a tolerable understanding and a thousand [pounds] a year.

Nancy

You are a rose, but set with sharpest spine;
You are a pretty bird that pecks at me;
You are a little squirrel on a tree,
Pelting me with the prickly fruit of the pine;
A diamond, torn from a crystal mine,
Not like that milky treasure of the sea,
A smooth, translucent pearl, but skillfully
Carved to cut, and faceted to shine.

If you are flame, it dances and burns blue;
If you are light, it pierces like a star
Intenser than a needlepoint of ice.
The dexterous touch that shaped the soul of you,
Mingled, to mix, and make you what you are,
Magic between the sugar and the spice.

Elinor Wylie

Sleep Well, My Dear

Sleep well, my dear, sleep safe and free;
The holy angels are with thee,
Who always see thy Father's face,
And never slumber, nights nor days.

Martin Luther

'The Wild, Barbarian Vacation Hours'

Dorothy Thompson's mother died when the famous author and journalist was a girl of seven. Succeeding her mother was her Aunt Elizabeth —the "Aunt Lizzie" of the reminiscence below, in which Miss Thompson remembers childhood rebellions familiar to any daughter:

Why did we so love [Aunt Lizzie] (though we sometimes shook impotent fists behind her back) that when we get together today, parents and grandparents ourselves, we always speak of her and the thought of her always makes us grin?

For one thing "she saw right through us." It was perfectly futile to lie to Aunt Lizzie. "Now that you've finished that cock-and-bull story," Aunt Lizzie would say (she was rather given to clichés), "what really happened?" Aunt Lizzie, though, didn't seem to think the cock-and-bull story a terrible crime. She *expected* it. She knew we were natural liars. She *understood* us. That was a comfort. Aunt Lizzie never believed you to be better than you were! And anticipating the worst, she was sometimes agreeably surprised!

Aunt Lizzie, also, was as prompt with rewards as with punishments. When I got a report card with four A's we had ice cream and angel food cake for supper, in my honor, and she didn't chide me for being rather smug about the achievement. . . .

Where, in this ordered and benevolently controlled life, did we work off our "tensions" and "unblock our aggressions"?

We worked them off in the streets, woods, fields, back lots, woodsheds and barns of the small towns where we lived. Supervised *play* was confined to a neighbor's occasional glance from a sitting room window. We expressed part of our rebellion against law by defying the laws of nature—jumping out of tall haylofts with an umbrella for a parachute, trying to walk the

tight rope of a knife-edged roof-tree, skating on thin ice and falling through, riding farm horses bareback and being thrown, negotiating icy hills with bobsleds and running into wagon teams. . . .

Out of doors and among ourselves we led our natural life, surcharged, quarrelsome, wild, imaginative, and secret—from adults. The hut we built in the woods, the cave-rooms excavated in snow, the secrets we told each other, the raids we made on orchards and melon patches, the incantations we chanted like witches in the church cemetery firmly believing they would cause the demise of some particular adult against whom we had sworn vengeance. Yet, with it all, the sense of wonder, sometimes amounting to ecstasy, at the mysterious beauty of the world around us—conscious in fleeting moments of the loveliness of skunk cabbage in April, the miracle of the showy lady's-slipper in June, the splendor of the autumnal maple tree. After all the wildness, bringing a bouquet of field flowers home to arrange in a vase, for father's study.

In the wild, barbarian vacation hours of our lives, we did many things of which our parents would not approve, and learned many things in a very rude, coarse way. It was a curiously dual life: the kind but firm severity of home and school; the unbridled private and herd life outside their walls—a combination of healthful care and healthy neglect.

But they complemented each other.

When we came home, exhausted, to have our wounds bound up (matter-of-factly, "If you *will* do such things, you must take the consequences," and ouch, the iodine!) home was shelter and haven. Then we were grateful—grateful for hot gingerbread; for the twinkle of a cozy fire; for father's kind steady face, and the noble stories he read us, creating our heroes; for Aunt Lizzie's calm voice of authority; for the cool, clean bed; for peace and security. Grateful, in short, for order and civilization, which tangibly paid off.   *Dorothy Thompson*

To My Daughter

Bright clasp of her whole hand around my
     finger,
My daughter, as we walk together now,
All my life I'll feel a ring invisibly
Circle this bone with shining: when she is grown
Far from today as her eyes are far already.

Stephen Spender

Her Favorites

My favorite dress
I must confess
Is not my red or blue or pink
(They're fine, I think),
But I like climbing trees and walls—
My favorite dress is overalls!
My favorite hat has nothing on it;
It's just my everyday sunbonnet.
My favorite summer shoes, you say?
Ha! I go barefoot all the day!

Mattie Lee Hausgen

'I Love You Very Much'

Author Cornelia Otis Skinner's father, Otis Skinner, was a celebrated actor and often away from home. Here he writes his young daughter after hearing that she had been ill:

Beloved Person:

I did not know when I wrote and asked you about Hallowe'en that you were still in bed. If I had, I should not have been so mean.

I really don't know why we get sick at the wrong time. I really don't know why we get sick at all. If I could answer that mystery I should be as wise as God and it isn't given to any of us down on this earth to be as wise as that, is it? Perhaps when you grow up and become a nice velvet-cheeked, snowy-haired, bright-eyed old lady you will know more about it. . . . I'm sure your dense-minded Daddy cannot tell . . . not now!

I remember I used to get sick at the wrong time. Once when the school term was coming to an end (and they *were* long terms when I was a kiddie) I was looking forward to the first day of my vacation because my mother had promised me I could go barefoot . . . and I *did* go barefoot. But I hadn't been without my shoes more than a few hours when I put my little heel on a cruel piece of slate and nearly tore it off. The doctor had to sew it up and I had to go to bed and stay there over two weeks. *And it was Vacation!* I don't think I should have minded so much if school term had still been on. (I'll tell you a secret . . . DON'T YOU TELL MOTHER!!) I was a dreadfully lazy scholar!

. . . So you mustn't be discouraged, but do as you always have done and you will find your joys will come in some other time. We always have just so much joy in our lives. We are like pitchers . . . we hold just so much: and sometimes we overflow and sometimes we are emptied out . . . and sometimes they take us and wash us out with soap because we have gotten dirty.

Well, dearie, this is a long letter for me to write you. Perhaps it is because I have lots of time in Louisville waiting for a train. Or perhaps it is because I love you very much.   *Fajie*

Oh, My Hazel-Eyed Mother

Oh, my hazel-eyed mother,
I looked behind the mulberry bush
And saw you standing there.
You were all in white
With a star on your forehead.

Oh, my hazel-eyed mother,
I do not remember what you said to me,
But the light floating above you
Was your love for your little girl.
                    Hilda Conkling
              (Written at the age of seven)

The Real Penalty

In his Autobiography, *Mark Twain remembers his daughter Susy's temper, and one result of it:*
As a child Susy had a passionate temper; and it cost her much remorse and many tears before she learned to govern it, but after that it was a wholesome salt and her character was the stronger and healthier for its presence. It enabled her to be good with dignity; it preserved her not only from being good for vanity's sake but from even the appearance of it. . . .

In the summer of 1880, when Susy was just eight years of age, the family were at Quarry Farm, on top of a high hill, three miles from Elmira, New York, where we always spent our summers in those days. Hay-cutting time was approaching and Susy and Clara were counting the hours, for the time was big with a great event for them; they had been promised that they might mount the wagon and ride home from the fields on the summit of the hay wagon. This perilous privilege, so dear to their age and species, had never been granted them before. Their excitement had no bounds. They could talk of nothing but this epoch-making adventure now. But misfortune overtook Susy on the very morning of the important day. In a sudden outbreak of passion she corrected Clara—with a shovel or stick or something of the sort. At any rate, the offense committed was of a gravity clearly beyond the limit allowed in the nursery. In accordance with the rule and custom of the house, Susy went to her mother to confess and to help decide upon the size and character of the punishment due. It was quite understood that as a punishment could have but one rational object and function—to act as a reminder and warn the transgressor against transgressing in the same way again—the children would know about as well as any how to choose a penalty which would be rememberable and effective.

Susy and her mother discussed various punishments but none of them seemed adequate. This fault was an unusually serious one and required the setting up of a danger signal in the memory that would not blow out nor burn out but remain a fixture there and furnish its saving warning indefinitely. Among the punishments mentioned was deprivation of the hay-wagon ride. It was noticeable that this one hit Susy hard. Finally, in the summing up, the mother named over the list and asked, "Which one do you think it ought to be, Susy?"

Susy studied, shrank from her duty, and asked, "Which do you think, mamma?"

"Well, Susy, I would rather leave it to you. *You* make the choice yourself."

It cost Susy a struggle and much and deep thinking and weighing—but she came out where anyone who knew her could have foretold she would:

"Well, mamma, I'll make it the hay wagon, because, you know, the other things might not make me remember not to do it again, but if I don't get to ride on the hay wagon I can remember it easily."

In this world the real penalty, the sharp one, the lasting one, never falls otherwise than on the wrong person. It was not *I* that corrected Clara but the remembrance of poor Susy's lost hay ride still brings *me* a pang—after twenty-six years. *Mark Twain*

'I Shall Send the Sheriff After You'

Often away from his home at Monticello, in Virginia, President Thomas Jefferson enjoyed correspondence with his daughters and grandchildren. Here he chides a favorite granddaughter, Eleanor Randolph, age eight, for not responding to his letters:

Miss Eleanor W. Randolph to Th. Jefferson

1805 May 21		Dr.
To a letter which ought to be written once in every three weeks while I am here, to wit from Jan. 1, 1805, to this day, 15 weeks		5.
Feb 23		Cr.
By one single letter of this day's date		1.
Balance due from E. W. Randolph to Th. J.		4.
		5

So stands the account for this year, my dear El-
len, between you and me. Unless it be soon paid
off I shall send the sheriff after you. I inclose
you an abundant supply of poetry, among
which you will find Goody Blake, which I think
you wanted. I will thank you if you will put on
your boots & spurs & ride to Monticello and in-
form me how my thorns live. This part of the
country is beautifying with them so fast that
every ride I take makes me anxious for those at
Monticello. Your Papa in his last letter informs
me the mumps have got into the family. Let me
know who have it and how all do. Kiss your
dear Mamma for me & shake hands with all the
little ones. Present me affectionately to your
Papa & accept *mes baismains* yourself.

Thomas Jefferson

DAUGHTERS

DREAMING

Prayer for a Daughter

God of men and God of nature,
Shape my daughter like the seasons.
Give her all the song of springtime
And the subtlety of April,
Generosity of summer,
Warmth and all the sweet fulfillment,
And the sparkling wit of autumn,
Color like October hillsides.
Lest her charms may be too many,
Give her something of the winter:
Stars and distances and silence,
Courage of the open spaces,
Wisdom of the waiting branches.
Don't forget to give her winter.

Esther Wood

Daydreams

Every young girl is a microcosm of the feminine world and holds within herself insoluble riddles which have puzzled mankind for countless centuries. There she sits, trim and decorative, in her undisturbed repose, and who can tell what is passing through her head? Is she thinking of a look some boy gave her yesterday, is she planning a new style for her hair, is she recalling some childhood incident, is she wondering what dress she will wear at next week's party, is she dreaming of her future, or is she, perhaps, all-unheedful of the ticking clock, just letting life flow through her in a resistless tide?

Richard Curle

Growing Up

Perhaps the surest way to tell when a female goes over the boundary from childhood into meaningful adolescence is to watch how long it takes her to get to bed at night. My own cross-over, which could be summed up in our family as "What on earth is Hildegarde *doing* in the bathroom?" must have occurred when I was a freshman in high school. Until then, I fell into bed dog-tired each night, after the briefest possible bout with toothbrush and washcloth. But once I'd become aware of the Body Beautiful, as portrayed in advertisements in women's magazines, my absorption was complete and my attitude highly optimistic. I too would be beautiful. *Hildegarde Dolson*

Thirteen

She enters with quiet assurance, offering
An afternoon miracle of bouffant locks,
Pale organdy gown instead of slacks . . .
Suffering
With shy delight the amazement
And admiration in our stare.

Entranced, we ponder
This sudden definite bloom
Like that on a small early apple,
The wonder
Of limbs ripened overnight into supple
Curves, the glossy burnish
Coating hair,
The luminous flesh.

"Glamor girl from skylarking moppet,"
We marvel, and the spell cracks.
A tongue of hot embarrassment licks
Her face,
The delicate sapling grace
Reverts to yesterday's unsure coltishness;
Dropping her eyes, digging one toe hard
Into the carpet,
She denies adolescence with a gruff word.

Florence Jacobs

If For Girls

If you can hear the whispering about you
And never yield to deal in whispers, too;
If you can bravely smile when loved ones
     doubt you,
And never doubt, in turn, what loved ones do;
If you can keep a sweet and gentle spirit
In spite of fame or fortune, rank or place,
And though you win your goal or only near it,
Can win with poise or lose with equal grace;
If you can meet with unbelief, believing,
And hallow in your heart, a simple creed,
If you can meet deception, undeceiving,
And learn to look to God for all you need;
If you can be what girls should be to mothers,
Chums in joy and comrades in distress;
And be unto others as you'd have the others
Be unto you—no more, and yet no less;
If you can keep within your heart the power
To say that firm, unconquerable "no";
If you can brave a present shadowed hour
Rather than yield to build a future woe;
If you can love, yet not let loving master,
But keep yourself within your own self's clasp,
And not let dreaming lead you to disaster
Nor pity's fascination loose your grasp;
If you can lock your heart on confidences

Nor ever needlessly in turn confide;
If you can put behind you all pretenses
Of mock humility or foolish pride;
If you can keep the simple homely virtue
Of walking right with God—then have no fear
That anything in all the world can hurt you—
And—which is more—you'll be a woman, Dear.

J. P. McEvoy

A Great Teacher Advises His Daughter

William James, the pioneer psychologist, was in Germany when he wrote this letter of advice to his 13-year-old daughter Margaret, at school in England:

Darling Peg—

Your letter came last night and explained sufficiently the cause of your long silence. You have evidently been in a bad state of spirits again. . . .

Now, my dear little girl, you have come to an age when the inward life develops and when some people (and on the whole those who have most of a destiny) find that life is not a bed of roses. Among other things there will be waves of terrible sadness, which last sometimes for days; and dissatisfactions with one's self, and irritation at others, and anger at circumstances and stony insensibility, etc., etc., which taken together form melancholy. Now, painful as it is, this is sent to us for enlightenment. It always passes off, and we learn about life from it, and we ought to learn a great many good things if we react on it rightly. (For instance, you learn how good a thing your home is, and your country, and your brothers, and you learn to be more considerate of other people, who, you now learn, may have their inner weaknesses and sufferings, too.)

Many persons take a kind of sickly delight in hugging it; and some sentimental ones may even be proud of it, showing a fine sorrowful kind of sensibility. Such persons make a regular habit of the luxury of woe. That is the worst possible reaction on it. . . . We mustn't submit to it an hour longer than we can help, but jump at every chance to attend to anything cheerful or comic or take part in anything active that will divert us from our mean, pining inward state of feeling. . . .

The worst of it often is that, while we are in it, we don't *want* to get out of it. We hate it, and yet we prefer staying in it—that is a part of the disease. . . . The disease makes you think of *yourself* all the time; and the way out of it is to keep as busy as we can thinking of *things* and of *other people*—no matter what's the matter with our self. . . .

Keep a merry heart—"time and the hour run through the roughest day"—and believe me ever your most loving   *William James*

Do's and Don'ts

In the midst of writing his third novel, Tender Is The Night, *the American author F. Scott Fitzgerald took time out to send this letter of fatherly advice to his 11-year-old daughter at camp:*

Dear Pie:

I feel very strongly about your doing [your] duty. Would you give me a little more documentation about your reading in French? I am glad you are happy—but I never believe much in happiness. I never believe in misery either. Those are things you see on the stage or the screen or the printed page, they never really happen to you in life.

All I believe in in life is the rewards for virtue (according to your talents) and the *punish-*

ments for not fulfilling your duties, which are doubly costly. If there is such a volume in the camp library, will you ask Mrs. Tyson to let you look up a sonnet of Shakespeare's in which the line occurs *Lilies that fester smell far worse than weeds.*

Have had no thoughts today, life seems composed of getting up a *Saturday Evening Post* story. I think of you, and always pleasantly; but if you call me "Pappy" again I am going to take the White Cat out and beat his bottom *hard, six times for every time you are impertinent.* Do you react to that?

I will arrange the camp bill.

Half-wit, I will conclude. Things to worry about:

Worry about courage

Worry about cleanliness

Worry about efficiency

Worry about horsemanship . . .

Things not to worry about:

Don't worry about popular opinion

Don't worry about dolls

Don't worry about the past

Don't worry about the future

Don't worry about growing up

Don't worry about anybody getting ahead of you

Don't worry about triumph

Don't worry about failure unless it comes
through your own fault
Don't worry about mosquitoes
Don't worry about flies
Don't worry about insects in general
Don't worry about parents
Don't worry about boys
Don't worry about disappointments
Don't worry about pleasures
Don't worry about satisfactions
Things to think about:
What am I really aiming at?
How good am I in comparison to my
contemporaries in regard to:
(a) Scholarship (b) Do I really understand
about people and am I able to get along with
them? (c) Am I trying to make my body
a useful instrument or am I neglecting it?

                 With dearest love, [Daddy]

P.S. My come-back to your calling me Pappy is
christening you by the word Egg, which im-
plies that you belong to a very rudimentary
state of life and that I could break you up and
crack you open at my will and I think it would
be a word that would hang on if I ever told it to
your contemporaries. "Egg Fitzgerald." How
would you like that to go through life with—

"Eggie Fitzgerald" or "Bad Egg Fitzgerald" or any form that might occur to fertile minds? Try it once more and I swear to God I will hang it on you and it will be up to you to shake it off. Why borrow trouble?

Love anyhow.

Occupied With Dreams

A moment comes in girlhood when the eyes are less occupied with the practical realities about them, than with dreams and visions of enchantment. The young girl has her reserves and her innate reticence, and often her nearest and dearest do not so much as lift a tiny edge of the curtain that drops between her and them. They speak of realities, prosaic affairs of the marketplace and of the present, while for her the true realities wear opal tints and are wreathed in violet mists. She is like the child who looks from the farmhouse door at the range of hills that rims the landscape, wondering what may lie on the other side.   *Margaret Sangster*

THE GLORY OF
WOMANHOOD

Behold the Woman

The land of make-believe is gone;
The dolls with which she used to play
Are sleeping high on closet shelves
For thus was childhood laid away.
But time transforms a little girl
By adding beauty, charm and grace;
And gives to her that special role
To make the world a better place.
Now proudly dressed in cap and gown
She clasps that all-important scroll.
Her smiling eyes express the thanks
For this—her long awaited goal.
May hope be always in her heart
And all her happy dreams come true;
Her zeal in serving others keep
The joy of living shining through.
We pray that life will treat her well
And keep her helpful, kind and good,
That she may justly claim the right
To wear the crown of womanhood!

Reginald Holmes

A Daughter's Glory

Accept your womanhood, my daughter, and rejoice in it. It is your glory that you are a woman, for this is why he loves you, he whom you love. Be gentle, be wise, as a woman is gentle and wise. Be ardent and love with a woman's ardor. Through your love, teach him what it means to be a man, a noble man, a strong man. Believe in him, for only through your belief can he believe in himself.

In our secret hearts, man and woman, we long above all else to know that the other, the one we love, knows what we are and believes in what we can be. Is this not romance? Yes, and the highest romance, investing the smallest detail of life with the color of joy.   *Pearl Buck*

The Terrible Cookware Caper

Every girl in the world could write a book entitled *Things My Mother Would Never Believe Even if I Told Her, Which I Never Would*. It would be a book about those awful trial-and-error lessons that loom large in every daughter's young life.

One chapter would have to be The Terrible Cookware Caper.

Since the beginning of time, girls going off to seek their fortunes have been warned and rewarned by mothers about the perils of listening to fast-talking door-to-door salesmen. But to no avail. You're always infinitely smarter than your mother. Off you go to the big city to be a career girl and await your first handsome salesman.

He's a young college student working his way through college. He's dashing, debonair, poised, and replete with dateable friends. When he offers to show you seven free gifts, you unhesitatingly invite him in for coffee and cake.

The wolf is now inside the camp. After a few minutes of small talk, he launches his dialogue. These are indeed seven wonderful gifts. No obligation. (Ah ha, you think. I did right.) And you may choose *two* of them, because you trapped your roommate into listening with you. You choose two.

So far, so good. But now he begins the Hope Chest routine, and you see a catch coming on strong. Resist, you tell yourself. Nobody, nobody ever falls for these lines. Remember what mother said. Be strong.

But the pan he describes is the most beautiful

pan in the history of mankind, and you gaze upon it with adoration. Not only does it shine like a mirror. It also practically prepares the food, cooks it, and washes itself afterward without your lifting a finger. Which sounds like a marvel, since you don't have any idea how to cook anyway.

You are captured. You are the great modern homemaker, whipping up gourmet dishes in knockout pots and pans. Blithely, you sign your life away.

As your salesman disappears out the door you find yourself left with no money and a set of the most beautiful cookware in captivity. Then, only then, do Mom's cautions come back. Dumb, you think. Really dumb. Never mind writing home. You'd never hear the end of it. It would be a family joke. Pay for the pans and shut up. Mother would never understand how the great career girl could pull such a stunt.

But maybe she would, at that.   *Jan Miller*

On the Eve of Her Wedding

My lovely daughter,

You are asleep now. I couldn't resist the impulse to look in on you a moment ago just as I have done a thousand times or more. This is the last night you will spend under our roof as merely our daughter. The next time you enter this house, you will be a wife (and a radiant one, I am confident).

You looked so beautiful at rehearsal tonight that I had to cry a little. Your father was crying, too. Inside, of course, where no one could see (he still thinks of you as his little girl, you know).

I watched you with the man whose life you will soon be sharing and I was suddenly reminded of the play-weddings of your childhood. And I thought of all the joys you have brought into my life since I carried you under my heart.

I remembered the way you used to look at me as I held you for a feeding or rocked you to sleep. Your shining eyes were so wide and so full of trust that it would almost break my heart. And I could almost see you as a lively little girl following me about the house, singing and chattering and begging to stir the cake batter or fold the towels or run the sweeper. And I remembered watching you grow into a lovely woman and sharing with you a new closeness and companionship.

Tomorrow you will begin woman's greatest and most fulfilling role. You will be a wonderful wife, I know, just as you have been a wonderful daughter. And it is my prayer that one day you will know the unique happiness that can only come from having a daughter as dear as you.

Your loving mother   *Barbara Burrow*

'Mr. X Is Too Old for You'

Poet Ogden Nash's daughter, visiting in Paris, was flattered by the company of an older man who proposed to her prior to obtaining a divorce from his wife. She wrote her father enthusiastically, then thought the situation over and wrote again the next day more reassuringly. Her father's response to the two letters:

Dearest Isabel,

I gather by now you have decided Mr. X is too old for you, as well as being a very silly man, but I am not pleased by the episode and I trust that by now you aren't either. The propensity of old men for flirting with young girls has been the object of coarse merriment since primeval days, as I should think your reading, if nothing else, should have told you.

You should be intelligent enough to know that in various eras of history it has been fashionable to laugh at morals, but the fact of the matter is that Old Man Morals just keeps rolling along and the laughers end up as driftwood on a sandbar. You can't beat the game, because morals as we know them represent the sum of the experience of the race. That is why it distressed me to find you glibly tossing off references to divorce. You surely have seen enough of its effects on your friends to know that it is a tragic thing even when forced on one partner by the vices of the other.

Read the marriage vows again—they are not just words, not even just a poetic promise to God. They are a practical promise to yourself to be happy. This I know from simply looking around me.

It bothers me to think that you may have sloppy—not sophisticated but sloppy—ideas about life. I have never tried to blind you to any side of life, through any form of censorship, trusting in your intelligence to learn of, and to recognize, evil without approving or participating in it. So please throw Iris March and all the golden doomed Bohemian girls away and be Isabel—there's more fun in it for you.

Keep on having your gay time, but just keep yourself in hand, and remember that generally speaking it's better to call older men Mister.

I love you tremendously,   Daddy

A Father's Tribute

The most famous lecturer of his time, Robert G. Ingersoll traveled most of the year and wrote back hundreds of letters to his daughters. On the occasion of the 34th birthday of his daughter Eva, he expressed his joy in the qualities he believed daughters should exhibit, qualities he found in Eva:

Dear Eva,

Thirty-four years of unbroken kindness, of cloudless sunshine, of perpetual joy, of constant love. Thirty-four years of happy smiles, of loving looks, of gentle words, of generous deeds. Thirty-four years of perfect days—perfect as the heart of June. Thirty-four years, a flower, a palm, a star; a faultless child, a perfect woman, wife and mother.

Wishes for Daughters

I want my daughters to be beautiful, accomplished, and good; to be admired, loved, and respected, to have a happy youth, to be well and wisely married, and to lead useful pleasant lives, with as little care and sorrow to try them as God sees fit to send.

To be loved and chosen by a good man is the best and sweetest thing which can happen to a woman; and I sincerely hope my girls may know this beautiful experience. It is natural to think of it, right to hope and wait for it, and wise to prepare for it; so that, when the happy time comes, you may feel ready for the duties and worthy of the joy.

My dear girls, I am ambitious for you, but not to have you make a dash in the world— marry rich men merely because they are rich, or have splendid houses, which are not homes because love is wanting. Money is a needful and precious thing—but I never want you to think it is the first or only prize to strive for. I'd rather see you poor men's wives, if you were happy, beloved, contented, than queens on thrones, without self-respect and peace.

Louisa May Alcott

Set at The Castle Press in Intertype Walbaum, a light
open typeface designed by Justus Erich Walbaum (1768-1839),
who was a type founder at Weimar.
Printed on Hallmark Eggshell Book paper.